COFFEE.
MONEY.
LOVE.

**DISCOVER WHAT YOU WANT,
WHAT YOU NEED,
AND WHAT YOU CAN'T LIVE WITHOUT**

Julie Colbrese

Copyright © 2022 by Hot Coffee Coaching LLC

All rights reserved. No part of this publication may be reproduced, distributed, or transmitted in any form or by any means, including photocopying, recording, or other electronic or mechanical methods, without the prior written permission of the author/publisher, except in the case of brief quotations embodied in critical reviews and certain other noncommercial uses permitted by copyright law. For permission requests, contact the author at hotcoffeecoaching.com.

Julie Colbrese/Hot Coffee Coaching LLC

Coffee. Money. Love. Discover what you want, what you need, and what you can't live without/Julie Colbrese — 1st ed.

ISBN 978-8-9855433-0-8

*For the family who made me
and the friends, colleagues, and clients
who made me better.*

Contents

Introduction 7
First, you're going to want to know what your values are .. 10
And it helps to know what you're good at 12
A note of advice on taking advice 14

COFFEE 17
What do you want? 18
What do you want on your pizza? 20
Am I a bad person for wanting so much? 22
What if I only know what I don't want? 24
What if I just want to be left alone? 26

MONEY 29
What do you need? 30
How much is enough? 32
I just lost my job, now what? 34
Am I in the right career? 36
I can't quit my job without having another job, right? ... 38

LOVE 41
What can't you live without? 42
Am I in the right relationship? 44
Am I enough? 46
Will anyone ever love me? 48
Is this all there is? 50

Acknowledgements 53
About the Author 55

Introduction

In 2017, my daughter and her family moved to Germany; I went with them. Our first stop was at a government office where they, as new residents, were required to register. The "welcome" sign, in German (of course), translated (quite rudely in my righteous American opinion) to:

What is your problem?

I believe what was meant was, "Oh you're new here! You look lovely and also exhausted. I notice you don't speak the language. How difficult that must be for you. What is it you want and how may we help you get it immediately and without fuss?"

Many of the clients who come to me do so without any idea of what they want. They just know they're unhappy, overwhelmed, stressed, or disappointed in themselves and the world around them. It's as if they've wandered up to that German information desk without the vaguest notion of what brought them there. They want to have more, but they don't know of what. They want to do less, but can't imagine what to have less of in their very full lives. They want something different, but not so different that it's scary or hard. Many people live their whole lives in a semi-unconscious state of dissatisfaction and disengagement. The people of France call it *ennui*, the feeling of being bored and unsatisfied with life. French can make anything sound romantic, but to live it can be excruciating.

I wrote this book because what I want is to inspire and support others to live their own version of a life well lived. What I need is to be deeply understood by myself and others. What I can't live without is to engage in provocative conversation.

Good conversation is the air I breathe.

Or, as a colleague astutely observed: conversation is your art.

So true I plan to stitch that on a pillow.

What you want, need, and can't live without can only be answered if you're willing to ask the questions, and only if you're willing to sit in the discomfort of not knowing… until you do. To that end, each entry in this book starts with a question that I'm often asked. To begin to answer it, I offer a story from my life and work that I hope will amuse, entertain, and inform you. Finally, after each entry, I'll leave you with an inquiry or prompt that you can use to journal around or ponder. That way, you can begin to coach yourself to your own version of success, satisfaction, and joy.

Start anywhere.

It is my deepest wish that where you end up is further than you ever imagined possible.

First, you're going to want to know what your values are

Part of discovering what you want is knowing what you care about. What matters most to you? Those are values. When our values are being met, whether consciously or unconsciously, we feel successful, satisfied, joyful, and loved. Values are personal. You get to decide what they are, and you don't have to justify them to anyone.

I have a friend who has a value he calls "champagne-pop." It's the feeling he gets when he's unexpectedly delighted. When that value is met by an unexpected delight, big or small, such as finding a crisp $20 bill in the street or getting the promotion he didn't even know he had coming, he feels joy, like the pop of a champagne cork.

One way to discover your values is to recall a time or event in your life when you were truly satisfied, proud, at peace, fully engaged, or alive. Everything felt right. For example, a memorable trip you took, a project you won, a challenge you overcame. What about it was so satisfying? Was it the people you were with? The feeling of success or accomplishment? The joy of being independent and free? When you look deeper, you'll likely discover the value(s) underneath. Your values, once identified, can serve as a kind of "North Star" to guide you to the people, places, and things that can make the difference between an unconscious life and a fully awakened life of success, satisfaction, and joy.

And it helps to know
what you're good at

If you're feeling like you're not good at anything, take some time over the next few weeks to take note of moments in your life and work where you do feel good. Notice when you're engaged in an activity and time slips away. Or when you find yourself smiling or humming a tune for seemingly no reason. You may be baking a cake and find yourself engrossed in the activity, and suddenly time has passed pleasantly without your knowing it. Make note of this cake baking. It doesn't mean you're going to be a baker (unless you are and that would be delicious), but it may be a clue. This is an exercise in discovery. Is it following a process with exacting detail? Is it delighting your family and friends? Is it throwing out the recipe and creating a cake from scratch? Your cake baking and mine may lead to two very different places: actually and metaphorically. The work to be done is to notice and get curious about the skills underneath the events and activities you truly enjoy.

A note of advice on taking advice

As a coach, I'm not in the advice or problem-solving business. This surprises a lot of people — namely my clients — who sometimes want me to tell them what to do. Believe me, it can sometimes take a great deal of self-management on my part not to give advice. In truth, I'm told I can be pretty bossy with my clients. The problem is other people's advice, while well-meaning, is rarely useful. Or as a colleague responds when asked his opinion: "If I were you, I would do this, and if you were me it would work."

We all wish for someone (almost) anyone to tell us what to do. Yet, other people aren't always the best resource for life decisions and, in some ways, may be among the worst. The better people know you — or think they know you — the more biased they may be. People who know you well may unconsciously be personally invested in your staying just the way you are. Although they may mean well, they likely want to keep you safe, steady, and close to home. In doing so, they may be unconsciously keeping you small.

Absolutely seek the advice of people you admire and respect and use it to inform the best decision made only by you only for you.

COFFEE

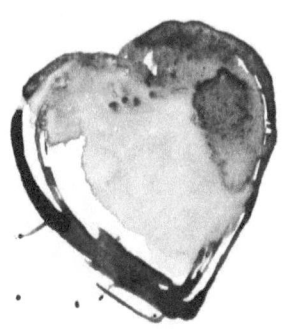

What do you want?

In 1989, a Starbucks opened a couple blocks from my place in Chicago. It wasn't the first in Chicago, that distinction went to 219 W. Jackson two years earlier, but it was the most conveniently located to me. I had been to a Starbucks in Seattle on a business trip and knew it was my kind of place. I went there for the first time on February 21, 1989, and then went back every day, twice a day for 23 years.

I know. It's bizarre to even know this. I love coffee.

You may be wondering what happened after that. I moved to a new neighborhood and switched to an independent coffee shop even closer to my house where I can see two (!) Starbucks from the front door. More often these days, I make my own coffee with an Italian moka pot balanced precariously on a too small stove top burner, a milk foamer, and a mason jar.

Knowing what I want has helped me to manage my time and resources to allow me to have exactly what I want — even at the ridiculous cost of a half hour of my life and nearly $10 or more a day — for more than three decades.

Note: please do not calculate the cost of my coffee. I've done the math myself and I'm so okay with it. Values, baby!

What do you want? What is it that you dream of that you are willing to invest time, trouble, and money into getting? Life is a series of negotiations; mostly with yourself.
Be ready for it.

What are some things you want? Practical or extravagant. Dream a little... or a lot.

What do you want on your pizza?

If you're someone who responds to requests for your opinion with "I don't know," "I don't care," or "whatever you want," let me assure you, you are not being accommodating, you are being tedious. Nothing is harder than trying to negotiate an outcome with someone who can't or won't state what it is they want. This is low-stakes asking for what you want and practicing here builds the muscle for other, more significant negotiations in your life. When someone asks, for example, what you want on your pizza, tell them and be willing to negotiate if there's a difference of opinion.

I once worked for a woman who held an all-staff meeting every Friday. She would stand at the head of a long conference table and lob rapid-fire questions at the staff on anything from current projects to wine to that morning's headlines. It was terrifying and I learned to, as she would say, bother to have an opinion.

In relationships and in life, we all have a responsibility to be interested and interesting.

Practice having an opinion and voicing it. Start by putting your stake in something; you can always negotiate from there.

Am I a bad person for wanting so much?

I live a life of privilege. I enjoy safety, security, and comforts to which not everyone has access; you may too. Yet, I still want for things: emotional, physical, and, yes, material (decorative tumbleweeds come to mind). It's not wrong to want.

Your wanting doesn't take away from others' needs or wants.

In fact, in some ways, your wanting may allow others to see what's possible. If what you want is legal and your means for going about getting it are ethical and not morally repugnant, go for it.

Practice wanting what you want. And want a lot.

What if I only know
what I don't want?

I grew up in the South Suburbs of Chicago. I have a vivid memory of riding my Schwinn Pixie through the tree-lined streets with a girlfriend when I was eight or nine-years-old. Back then the suburbs were advertised as "the best of both worlds": the convenience of the city combined with the wide-open spaces of the country. Even at eight, I knew that was some made-up marketing nonsense (fast forward to me making an entire career of marketing nonsense. Oops!) I didn't know what I wanted, but I knew the suburbs weren't for me.

I couldn't wait to get out.

Knowing and being able to articulate what you don't want can be as powerful as knowing what you do want. When there's conflict or dissonance in how you feel, look for the belief underneath. If the suburbs feel too bucolic, you may be unknowingly saying yes to the energy and aliveness of a more urban setting. I'm sure you've heard the expression: if it's not a "hell yes," it's a "hell no." If it's a hell no, what would make you say "yes?"

When considering work, life, or love, what's a "hell no" for you?

What if I just want to be left alone?

Every time I feel lonely or rejected or somehow slighted, I hear myself say (to myself, naturally): "I just want to be left alone." It's one of those lies we tell ourselves to protect our fragile selves when the very opposite is most true: I want to be included, encouraged, and loved. What I want to say is "come and get me," but it feels too vulnerable and too scary to ask for what I really want.

Once, in a heated argument, the man I was dating interrupted my rage to say softly: "I'm right here." It was the rightest thing anyone has ever said to me then or since.

When you're at your most vulnerable place, consider making yourself even more vulnerable by asking for what you really want. The ask may be hard, but the giving is easy: be with me, listen to me, love me.

MONEY

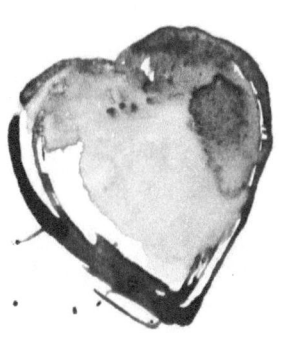

What do you need?

I love making money. I'm good at it. I don't know why. As a kid, I had the obligatory lemonade stand, but I didn't stop there. I put on musicals with full choreography in my garage, had toy sales, started a neighborhood newspaper, and put on a carnival, among other mini-entrepreneurial endeavors. When I turned 14, I got a "real" job at Baskin-Robbins for $1/hour (ONE DOLLAR AN HOUR!). When I turned 16, I got a car. With a job and a car, I felt powerful.

I have never not worked since.

I love to work.

I think I love to work because, even as a 14-year-old Baskin Robbins employee, I knew what the deal was: I do something you don't want to do; you pay me money.

Knowing what you need, whether financial, physical, intellectual, spiritual, or emotional is important.

What's it for you? What are you willing to work for?

How much is enough?

Some time ago, I was in a leadership training class where we had to enroll others in an idea or a cause we felt passionate about. I chose to speak about the concept of enough. When I was finished, someone offered the feedback that, while I was certainly well spoken and passionate, they didn't really understand the concept. Others agreed.

Exactly. My. Point.

There's an "American-style" clothing store in Germany called "More and More." It makes me laugh every time I walk by. It may be an American thing, I'm not sure, but it seems more is in our DNA.

On a pandemic-inspired family road trip to Montana, I picked up a medicine ball-sized tumbleweed on the side of the road. It was literally blocking traffic; cars were slowing and driving around it. I tossed it in the back seat and covered it with a blanket, *ET*-style, in case there's a law against exporting wild tumbleweeds (there is not). When I got home, I arranged it on a side table in my living room.

My first thought was, I freakin' love this tumbleweed; my second thought was, I need another one.

I assure you no one needs more than one decorative tumbleweed.

Figure out what you need. This is a math problem and I promise you can do it. What are the expenses, products, and services you must spend money on to be safe and healthy? Start there.

I just lost my job, now what?

Deep breath. I've worked with dozens of people who have lost their jobs either by their own shenanigans or by any number of circumstances that have found them employed one day and unemployed the next. No one — even the most miserable in their roles — likes it when employment doesn't end on their own terms and timing. If this is you, take a deep breath and put together a physical workout plan that starts now.

Seriously, out of work and out of shape should never go together.

Your physical and emotional health is your number one job now. Make a commitment to taking extra good care of yourself. If you've been meaning to stop smoking, start working out, sleep more, drink less.

Do. It. Now.

There will be plenty of time to write a resume, update your LinkedIn profile and start networking. First, get healthy, fit, and strong. The structure will give you focus. You'll build much needed confidence, and you'll look f-ing hot, and that will make you feel like you own the universe.

What's it going to be? Choose a healthy activity and get busy.

Am I in the right career?

During the pandemic an organization with which I am affiliated had an immediate and somewhat desperate need for people to perform technical hosting duties for online classes. I was an experienced video conference user — or so I thought — and happily volunteered. To say I was horrible in this (volunteer) role would be an understatement. It was a clear example of "you don't know what you don't know." It may be the hardest thing I've ever done in my life. I did it exactly once and quit. I'm not sure anything good came from the experience for either party, but notably I came away with this insight: my version of hell is to work hard at something I neither care about nor enjoy.

I am no stranger to hard work, and I have many examples of working hard to improve myself in any number of ways intellectually, emotionally, physically, but to put time and effort into something that doesn't have meaning and/or isn't enjoyable (AND doesn't make me money) is truly torturous.

Don't. Do. It.

Consider whether you are interested and engaged enough in your current career to want to do what it takes to advance or get better at it.

I can't quit my job without having another job, right?

Not only can you quit your job without having another job, it may be the exact right thing for you to do. Some people need to create the space to consider their next move. If this is you, do whatever you have to do to grab the time you need. Shockingly, many people I work with don't take all their vacation or PTO days. If this is you, and you're wondering how you'll find the time to look for a new job, contact HR immediately and request those days off. If you're feeling bold, you may even negotiate a sabbatical.

Now. Right now.

If it's still not enough, you may choose to quit.

When making a conscious decision from employed to unemployed you may want to consider the difference between risky and reckless. Risky is quitting knowing it may take you longer than you planned to find an ideal or acceptable job. You may need to dip into savings. You may need to move back in with your parents or get a roommate temporarily.

Reckless is quitting with no means of supporting yourself.

One more note on when you might quit a job without having another job. If you are in a horrible work environment that is negatively impacting your health or safety, please get out. If you were in an abusive personal relationship, no one would expect you to stay until you find another partner. A truly toxic work environment — not "Morgan in accounting is mean" — can be equally damaging to your health and safety.

Realistically assess your ability to look for a job while you have a job and consider if quitting would be risky or reckless.

LOVE

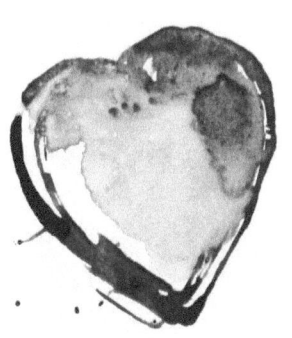

What can't you live without?

If recent history has taught us anything, I hope it is that love can look a lot of different ways and come in some truly remarkable packages. If you are at a point in your life where love as you imagined it has been elusive, I encourage you to broaden your definition of love.

Love can be tricky.

I became widowed at age 33. It wasn't the love story either of us had planned. You might think things could only go up from unexpected death, but turns out that's not entirely true. That is not to say I haven't loved since, but love has looked a lot of different ways, sometimes challenging, sometimes complicated, most often experienced through family, friends, colleagues, clients, a dog, a coffee, a hard workout, a good book.

Some years ago, I wrote a blog post titled "This is why you don't kill yourself." It was about experiencing joy alone at home with bad TV (The *Twilight* movie) and good Thai (Tiparos in Lincoln Park; try the Tom Yum Soup). Love is like that. It shows up in unexpected ways in unexpected places.

It's not about who you love, it's about how you love, and like most lessons it starts with you.

What do you love about yourself? Make a list. Make a long list. Be generous and kind. And in what unexpected ways do you experience love?

Am I in the right relationship?

Once, as a single parent, out of anxiety and desperation, I asked my then teenaged son to read a text exchange between a guy I was dating and me.

"Here! Read these!" I said, shoving my phone at him. "Tell me if you think this guy likes me".

My son, a relentless truth-teller, held up his hands and shuffled backwards out of the room.

"I don't need to read it, Mom. You're amazing and successful and beautiful and you're wasting your time trying to figure out if some dude likes you. That's bullshit."

I agree (and not just with the parts about me).

If you find yourself, like me, asking others for their opinion on your relationship, you're probably in the wrong relationship. If you find yourself replaying and parsing every conversation or text exchange (also like me), you're probably in the wrong relationship. If you feel anxious or bored or annoyed or if you feel nothing at all, you're probably in the wrong relationship. If you feel like you're doing all the work or if you think you care about the other person more than the other person cares for, considers, or does for you, you're probably in the wrong relationship. If you're embarrassed by this person, you're probably in the wrong relationship. If you turned to read this page first, you're probably in the wrong relationship.

I don't know this for sure, but you sure do.

Ask yourself that question again and listen quietly for the whisper of what you already know is true.

Am I enough?

Yes. Yes, you are.

Consider telling yourself this often and with conviction: I am enough.

Will anyone ever love me?

Some of us grew up not sure if we are lovable and worthy of love. It's a bitch, for sure.

I can tell you, without a doubt, you are lovable and worthy of love. Don't take my word for it though; love starts close to home. Find a mirror and take a good soft look at yourself. There you go. Look at that beauty. Now, love that person up. Gaze deeply into those eyes. Give a little wink. Blow a kiss.

Repeat as necessary.

Is this all there is?

I don't know. Maybe? Your "this" may be all there is, but it's up to you. Is it enough? It very well may be and, if you're awake and living with intention, relax and enjoy what you have created. Well done!

On the other hand, do you want something more, better, different? Whatever it is, you won't be able to think your way to what's next. You're going to have to do the sometimes hard work of figuring out what's underneath and what's holding you back, and then get yourself into action. Move. Do something.

Maybe start by identifying one thing you want. Right now.
Now, go get it.
You can do it.
I believe in you.

Acknowledgements

I am blessed to have had two successful and satisfying careers. First, in a marketing agency where I had the pleasure of working with some of the most clever, creative, and interesting people I've ever met, many of whom remain among my closest friends. While there, I worked for and with my dear friend and business partner, Jay Farrell. Jay taught me everything I know about being a good leader and a good person. To this day, I would follow him anywhere.

My second career, and the work in the world I do today, is as a Co-Active Coach. I am deeply grateful to Karen and Henry Kimsey-House and the Co-Active Training Institute for everything I learned and continue to learn as a participant and faculty member (dreams do come true). Check it out and hire your own co-active coach. https://coactive.com

Finally, to Tessa and Ben. Thank you for making me believe I am the best parent in the world by being the two people who love me the most. Love you more!

About the Author

Julie Colbrese earned Certified Professional Co-Active Coach (CPCC) distinction from the Co-Active Training Institute, where she is a member of the faculty, and Master Certified Coach (MCC) distinction from the International Coach Federation. She is a regular contributor to Forbes and a frequent national and international speaker on topics including coaching, communication, and creativity.

Based in Chicago, Julie works with clients everywhere over the phone and over coffee. For more information about Hot Coffee Coaching, visit: www.hotcoffeecoaching.com.

www.ingramcontent.com/pod-product-compliance
Lightning Source LLC
Chambersburg PA
CBHW020653060526
44119CB00069B/27